60-MINUTE MARKETING

THE COTTON T-SHIRT

A beginner's guide to developing a breakout brand

LORI THOMAS

www.60minutemarketing.com

ISBN-13: 978-1983511202
ISBN-10: 198351120X

Cover design and graphics by Don Donaudy, Jr.

CONTENTS

What's with this title?

If what you are about to learn in this opening chapter makes you angry, then let me be the first to congratulate you. You picked up the right book.

Settle in and prepare to accept the hard-fact that every purchase decision you have ever made in your life was the result of manipulation. Let me be clear that the negative connotation that word typically carries is not intended to in this case. Truth is, branding is just one form of manipulation, albeit a socially acceptable one when attributing it to the wonderful yet subjective world of marketing.

---

ma·nip·u·late - mə´nipyə,lāt/
verb
1. handle or control (a tool, mechanism, etc.), typically in a skillful manner.
2. control or influence (a person or situation) cleverly, unfairly, or unscrupulously.

Clearly, unfair and unscrupulous practices have no place in your business, however a clever mindset and skillful approach certainly do. Developing and executing a smart branding campaign requires a solid plan. This beginner's guide is intended to take you on that explorative journey, one I have been on for my own businesses as well as with many clients throughout my career from small mom-and-pop shops to major international giants.

Back in high school when I was considering paths for my collegiate course of study that would hopefully lead to a prosperous lifelong career, I was repeatedly advised by mentors to search for and identify areas of my life that I was truly passionate about. Having always been energized when debating all types of concepts and ideas and motivated by the goal of proving any point, my first thought was that I should be an attorney. Further self-assessment helped me uncover that I was also quite intrigued by people and why they did what they did in any given situation. What was their motivation or subconscious response that lead them to make a certain decision or to behave a certain way? I considered abandoning the attorney idea and opting instead for a career in psychology so I could study and practice that fascinating art of human behavior.

When decision time came around, I chose the advertising field. For me, it was the perfect combination of psychology and law all wrapped up in a creative little package. First, one researches and uncovers what motivates consumers to purchase certain goods and services. Next, one formulates a convincing argument that their brand is the best one to buy. The psychology of consumer motivation combined with a public trial to convince members of the buying jury that my version of the story is the obvious answer... bam! That's advertising. So, the decision was made and it's been a fun ride. Let's get something out of the way right upfront regarding any point in my career when you may have been someone I was targeting. I am about to come clean on my steps taken in attempt to convince you to choose the brand that I was pitching you to purchase. If I was successful, my hope is that you will be okay with it and consider using these same strategies in your new business venture to communicate with your prospects. In other words, the view from where I sit looks like we're even.

My decision for the name of this guide came about because I believe that a cotton t-shirt is a very basic item that most people own therefore it's safe to assume that many of you have made a purchase decision about this very common article of clothing at some point in your life.

Do you realize that billions of dollars are spent every year by advertisers competing to convince consumers to buy their cotton t-shirts? Billions of dollars. Every year. To manipulate you to buy this very basic product.

Maybe it's white, black, pink, whatever color it is doesn't matter. Let's just recall a day that you shopped for a 100% cotton t-shirt and the one you purchased was perfect for you and got the job done. Where did you buy it? How much did you pay for it, and why? Whatever your reasons, you didn't make those decisions by yourself. Before you even stepped out of your home or turned on your computer to shop, you were already manipulated into believing what the best decisions would be regarding where to make this purchase and how much to pay for it. Your only job was to go and execute the plan the successful advertiser laid out for you. Of the following two examples, identify which consumer you relate to most.

Customer #1 bought his t-shirt at Billy's Big Box store for $9.99. He believes the value proposition was spot on and anyone paying even a penny more for the same exact 100% cotton t-shirt anywhere else is not a smart shopper like he clearly is. Customer #2 bought his 100% cotton t-shirt at a name brand store for $29.99, same size and color, but his has that store's brand logo visible on the front left pocket and because he considers himself to be a very stylish dresser who only wears the best, this purchase validates he made the right choice. Both stores were successful in manipulating their target into believing the 100% cotton t-shirt each of them had hanging on the rack for sale was the better choice than the same 100% cotton t-shirt being sold at the other store. Two t-shirts, same material, same color, vastly different price points, yet two successful sales. The magic for both conversions can be found in the branding messages that were sent, received, and believed by each customer well in advance of t-shirt shopping day.

Although possible, it is highly unlikely that both consumers went to both stores to compare the 100% cotton t-shirts against each other to eventually decide on which one they were going to purchase. Instead, like good little shopping puppets, each consumer flawlessly completed the buying tasks they didn't even know were assigned to them by the branding puppeteers. Those are the geniuses who had been pulling both consumers' shopping strings for days, weeks, months and possibly even years to remind each of them of their pre-programmed beliefs and where they will shop as a result of those beliefs when the need arises for any item they offer. Cotton t-shirt included.

You have been manipulated this same way throughout your entire life when making purchase decisions similar in nature to this one. Of course, when injecting variables into a product or service that can support and rationalize varying price-points we are talking a completely different branding game than illustrated in the cotton t-shirt example. There are obvious differences between the feel of sheets with a 500 versus 5,000 thread count, or the proven performance of a car engine that can zero-to-60 in, well, whatever versus whatever seconds.

When developing your master brand plan there is much to consider and together we will begin the process of identifying and then mixing the right ingredients to create a solid foundation for your brand to build upon. It is possible that you can have a product that is technically inferior to your competitors and still be the top-selling brand in your category, by a lot! It is also possible to be the top-selling brand in your category because all other options are, in fact, inferior to yours in a provable way. Even still, it is possible to have a product that is exactly the same as your competitors just like a cotton t-shirt, yet your sales could be more than double your closest rival. In each of these scenarios, creating the right story for your customer is where the branding game starts.

So, let's play.

Who are you?

The Cotton T-Shirt

The word you is a relative one. It can literally mean 'you' if you are in fact what is being sold like a fitness trainer, chiropractor, interior designer, private chef, attorney or life coach. Or 'you' can be your product or service being offered for sale. Determining who and what you are and why you are relevant to your target consumer are the first critical steps in brand planning that cannot be overlooked, otherwise you will just be talking to yourself and wasting precious time and money.

Let's agree that the world does not need another brand of toothpaste. For those of my generation, Crest was the family toothpaste to prevent cavities because fluoride was all the rage and giving Gleem a run, Close-Up was for couples seeking fresh breath, Aquafresh came in with a combination of both attributes, Colgate remained a giant with the first collapsible tube, and Pearl Drops Tooth Polish was considered the whitening breakthrough.

Today you can stand in the toothpaste isle at your favorite store anywhere and staring back at you is a myriad of options that take up about 10 feet of isle space three shelves deep. Even with all of those brands quietly standing army-style on display fighting for your almighty dollar, you have not gone in blind to make this purchase and are in no way overwhelmed by all of these choices. Resulting from the preceding mental and emotional manipulation of you that has already taken place, you arrive at the store armed with a firm set of desires you wish to see fulfilled and will cast your vote via the purchase of the toothpaste brand that best meets your criteria. So you think.

Your desires could be fresh breath, organic composition, minty taste, extreme whitening, sensitive on the nerves, any combination of these or something completely different. The shelf of 50 options for you to choose from has already been dramatically reduced to five that you instinctively gravitate to because you have been preconditioned by the advertisers to search specifically for the shiny hook they dropped into your ocean. From there you choose a brand and if the experience is positive you will repeat that purchase in the future.

If you are a college student who has used toothpaste all of your life but suddenly find yourself having to make this purchase for the first time, it is highly probable that your instinct will be to simply buy whatever was in your house before you moved away to college or to choose the cheapest one on the shelf because most college kids are broke, and you may be as well. It is also just as likely that although toothpaste ads have been in front of your face in recent years you may finally start to notice them for the first time now that you've entered the toothpaste consumer market. Rest assured that advertisers have been spending a lot of money planting seeds in your head while they were waiting for you to arrive. At the point when you assume your post as an engaged consumer in this industry, odds are that you will choose a brand completely different from the one that was in your childhood home for all of your formative years. As a young millennial you realize that you are looking for something from your toothpaste that your parents were not. You will eventually become a loyal purchaser of your new brand and likely call home and attempt to school your parents about the toothpaste you now use that is far better than the one they chose for you when you were younger. In addition to my professional analysis of this example, I may or may not be speaking from personal experience. Not to digress.

To pinpoint exactly who your brand will be in the public eye requires that you briefly step away from your self-proclaimed awesomeness to identify every negative inherent in your product while consequently conducting a thorough analysis of your competitors' strengths. At the conclusion of this exercise you should be able to visually chart the holes in the market which may actually present you with some unique opportunities you hadn't thought of. Regardless, this will help you determine where your brand fits in the marketplace and what path you should explore going down to best position it.

What problem does your product solve? Keep in mind that a problem does not have to be a negative thing. At one time in my past I had no idea that looking for a pay phone was an inconvenient and laborious task. Quite the contrary because I believed finding a phone booth was a modern convenience! Portable and then cellular phones did not technically solve a problem, they enhanced an existing out-of-home communication convenience and then ultimately revolutionized human behavior which resulted in the demise of out-door pay phones. I'd say it is a pretty big deal if even Superman is affected by a revolutionary new product. Even though I did not have a problem with pay phones, I absolutely needed to purchase "the new solution" when it became available. I was manipulated into believing I had to have a cell phone because my life would some-how be better, so I followed marketing orders and dil-igently sought out to make my purchase having been convinced that I would enjoy that better life because of this action. I have continued to repeat this process over and over again as the manipulation train continued down the tracks with the follow-up launches of the latest and greatest models offering newly developed features no average brain could conceive. Funny. The small per-centage of people on this planet who still do not have cell phones seem happier and freer than myself who is supposed to be living a better life due to my participa-tion as an active consumer in the cell phone market.

If you believe your product is revolutionary like this, I highly suggest you spend a great deal of time eval-uating the lifestyle change you expect your consumers to have as a result of using your product and prepare your-self for a battle much larger than just selling the item. In essence, your product needs to change a behavior, and change is hard. You must uncover and demonstrate all the possible ways your product will change the buyers' life and paint a very clear picture of what that looks like. Remember that although you have been living

your product's development for some time, the public has no concept yet of what it is and does not understand your language. Like teaching a baby to walk, an adult cannot simply speak to the baby and explain how to stand up and put one foot in front of the other to become independently mobile. This would result in a baby's blank stare back at the adult as the baby continues to sit idly on the floor. That baby is your customer who does not understand your concept or what you are saying. You must take them gently by both hands, lift them up on their feet, and once they are steady you will guide them through the actual process of walking until the lightbulb goes off and they're hooked! That's behavior change. That's a sale. And it may even become a movement if you do it right.

Maybe you are preparing to launch in the most common scenario of a 'me too' product that will be a new option entering an already existing sector and said products in that sector do solve a real problem. Body aches and pains of any kind are an obvious example of problem-solution. In this case there are many products that claim to solve this problem so why don't they all just say they relieve pain and leave it at that? That's not enough, that's why. No differentiation exists to guide consumers to their decision. If someone wants pain relief fast they will gravitate to buy Brand A. If a consumer is seeking pain relief that lasts the longest they are more inclined to purchase Brand B. Both products are in the pain relief category and do relieve pain, yet the puppeteers have carefully and clearly differentiated their product from each other, the competition. *Carefully and clearly.* If you are entering the market with Brand C, then consumers need to know what makes you different and be convinced that your unique differentiation is the best choice. "Hi there, I am a new pain reliever with fancy packaging so pick me" is not going to cut it because you have absolutely no manipulation power without a compelling argument. So, have an argument. It's called brand differentiation.

Now, let's discuss the lifestyle sale for those of you where direct comparison of your product versus competitors is nearly impossible so your brand differentiation becomes about the end user. What? Sure, look at the entire fragrance industry. We do not see ads saying a product smells better than another or smells the best. Perfume and cologne products are all about scents, yet it is difficult to recall any brand that even talks about its actual scent when marketing! Here, the brand is the end user or better yet, what the end user relates to and how they perceive themselves or desire to be perceived by others. Naturally, one needs to like the scent, however the fact is that a consumer will not even pick up a bottle to test the scent if they do not already relate with the brand. For men seeking a celebrity cologne it is unlikely that the same consumer would pick up and test the fragrances sold by 50 Cent, Pitbull and Jay-Z as well as those sold by Antonio Banderas and Tim McGraw. How about the cologne sold by the New York Yankees? We all know two different people in our lives who would absolutely wear it and never wear it, regardless of what it smelled like. Then there are fashion branded perfumes like Chanel, Donna Karan, Calvin Klein, Dolce & Gabbana and celebrity branded options offered by stars like Jennifer Aniston and Drew Barrymore. Ladies must identify with the fashion or like the actress first before they would even consider picking up the test bottle to smell it. Consumers are already pre-sold on the umbrella brand and the lifestyle it represents so they are more inclined to consider any product introduced into that brand's product line.

Whether you are branding a solution product, new and improved game changer, never-seen-before idea, a 'me too' option, or yourself as the prize, define your truth and then move on to developing your brand posture which is the second but equally important component of identifying who you are.

Brand posture rounds out the offering story. Brands are inanimate objects, yet the successful ones absolutely have personalities. Think about it. How can a box on a shelf or a logo on the wing of an airplane have a personality? The reason they do is a result of the mind manipulation that convinced you of it. I won't even show you the logos, but I assure you these brand personalities come through loud and clear when written in just plain type. Southwest, friendly. Apple, smart. Firestone, reliable. Rolex, elusive. Ford, tough. Downy, cuddly. Nike, victorious. In actuality, southwest is just a direction, apple is a fruit, Firestone and Ford are family names,

Nike was a goddess, and the others are not even words in the English language. Resulting from years of genius marketing these brands were created with distinct personalities that you believe to be so because you were told it.

When you figure all of this out for your brand, it really gets exciting. Let's keep going.

Who cares?

Now that you are even more excited about developing your brand differentiation, basically your consumer could care less. Sorry.

From the moment you wake up until the moment you go to sleep you are probably consumed with thoughts of your business. It is imperative that you consistently remind yourself that your consumer is not even remotely concerned with you or your product because they have their own life they are trying to live and unless and until you can demonstrate your relevance, you will be completely ignored.

A common mistake of rookie marketers is believing their product is the best thing ever invented and everyone in the world should see it as clearly as they do the first time it is presented to them. This often causes a marketer to vomit on their prospects and that typically comes in the form of a full-page ad that looks like a college thesis paper or an aggressive salesperson that won't stop talking about how great the product is for their customer without even knowing anything about the customer in the first place. Consider yourself as the prospect in those scenarios. You would have likely turned the page, or told the salesperson to take a walk. You must be relevant. You must be consistent. And you must be patient. Let's begin with relevance.

Get your ideal target customer down to one person and give him or her a name. Know everything about this person which requires a great deal of research on your part. Know the age, what type of residence they live in, the things they may like to do, what type of employment they may have, if any. Recognize that I said your ideal customer, not all your customers. The ideal customer is the center of your world, the bullseye of the target. Your brand will naturally appeal to those with other characteristics in all circles around the bullseye but the goal here is to go straight to the center of the prospect pool and identify who your bullseye is. You cannot convince someone that you are relevant in their life if you do not know them.

Now do a little role playing as if your brand meets your prospect at a party and they are about to be introduced. There will be a first impression, an immediate sizing up to look for red flag warnings, and an evaluation if the personality aligns or clashes. Marriage rarely happens immediately following this 5-minute introduction, yet a decision is always made whether further conversation will be explored, or not.

If your brand shows up at the party completely disheveled (confusing identity) and stands silently and motionless in the middle of the room (no personality) you can predict that guests in attendance will not be interested in engaging with your brand (not relevant) resulting in no conversation (zero sales). Let's explore the flip side.

Your brand shows up in a custom-tailored suit with all appropriate accessories (clear identity) and immediately smiles, shakes hands and exchanges greetings with many in attendance (pleasant personality). Guests will likely be fine with an introduction to your brand (relevant through social validation) resulting

in conversation (potential for sale).

Next is consistency. If your brand shows up at party after party with the same people in attendance yet looks and acts totally different every time, then your brand will be regarded as a weirdo who is trying too hard. This is likely to result in a verdict of irrelevant by the party-goer jury until the real brand (please) stands up and a different decision can 'possibly' be made. In marketing, this typically looks like a company that tries all sorts of different ad messages, styles, and postures in the never-ending search for the one ad that will work. Consumers don't buy ads, they buy products that have convinced them of its relevancy in their life by consistently communicating their message in an engaging way.

As far as patience, ask yourself when the last time was that somebody told you a new idea just one time and you immediately set out without question to execute the idea. Maybe you've done this, but I hardly believe you make it a common practice. Don't expect this reaction from your prospects. Branding is a process, not an overnight sensation. Those that do it well see better long-term results than those that have temporary flash in the pan success and close down shop soon thereafter. Those that do it well don't rush out haphazardly into a market without doing the necessary due diligence and formulating a solid plan. As the plan unfolds it is monitored carefully to identify modifications and enhancements that can positively impact brand relevancy. Quitting after 24-hours on the market is not an option for

Consumers don't buy ads, they buy products that have convinced them of its relevancy in their life by consistently communicating their message in an engaging way.

these marketers because they know that any well-designed plan takes longer than 24-hours to unfold. Insert whatever timeframe you like for that statement, you get the point.

The value of testing

The Cotton T-Shirt

If you are absolutely certain that you are not talking to yourself and the brand strategy you have developed is a sure-fire hit, then no need to keep reading and I wish you the best of luck. For me, the communication testing phase has always been my favorite part of the campaign development process. Throughout my career this step has either confirmed with hard data that I was on the right track or saved me immeasurable dollars that would have been wasted had I opted to go with an all-in bet based solely on my personal opinion. I've been called a gambler at the Texas Hold'em table, but moves like that were always too rich for my bank account or my professional reputation too important to risk my clients' budgets. As with most things in life there are no guarantees with a tested marketing communication strategy, but educated plays are always better than empty guesses.

Prior to your brand's very expensive coming out party, put your marketing language in front of your prospects on a smaller scale first. The operative words there were your prospects. Not your mother or your best friend and certainly not your significant other. Your prospects. Chances are your loved ones will be encouraging and supportive and afraid to crush your dream with the slightest negative word so there is nothing to gain there. If they do happen to offer a challenging critique you are likely to respond emotionally because you'll feel that they do not understand what you are doing. This will result in an unwanted relationship problem you will need to deal with which has nothing to do with your business. Save yourself the lost rest from sleeping on the couch and instead find potential customers to test your pitch. Again, I may or may not be interjecting personal experience.

Your product is your product therefore this phase assumes you are all the way passed the research and development process for your product and you are ready with your go-to-market final version. Here, your testing is designed to identify the best way to communicate with prospects about your product. You are in search of the best language that tells your story (the differentiation and relevancy) and the tone of voice that will deliver it (the personality).

To run an effective communications test requires that you prepare varied options to put in front of your prospects. Varied options do not mean different colors in your advertising piece, that is not direct communication. Rather you must develop uniquely different ways of talking about your product to determine which language resonates best with your bullseye. There are many different ways to say the same thing. White is clear, or crisp, or pure, or angelic. Soft is comfortable, plush, soothing, or squishy. Your objective is to communicate the differentiating attribute via identification of the best words to use.

In addition to developing options you believe will work best you should also consider developing options you believe will not work at all. Including these options in your test will force the most effective method to naturally rise from the batch. Multiple options that have very similar language and the same tone will not produce the feedback you need to make an educated decision as the variances would be so miniscule your prospects will start nit-picking other things in search of something to give feedback on. This often leads to comments about font style or moving pictures to a different spot on the page, all of which are irrelevant at this stage and not what you are seeking feedback about.

Stay focused on developing options that will provide the opportunity for you to confirm and exclude different postures. Be open to surprises here and regularly check yourself that you are not pushing your internal idea that you've already decided was the right answer before you even started your test. Search for the best option and keep in mind that it may be different than the slam dunk you thought you had going in. If you are the inventor of your product that does not automatically make you the expert voice of your customer. Although you may have developed your product because of a personal experience it may turn out that your product's appeal is narrower or wider than you originally thought. You would naturally be a customer, but you may not be the bullseye. Do you want to make money, or do you want to be right? Kudos if you wind up achieving both but never assume that you know better than your customer. We all know what they say about those who assume.

Creativity injection

The Cotton T-Shirt

Many people are fascinated by the glamorous world of advertising because of the creativity witnessed during the best Superbowl parties. My husband and business partner in the national advertising agency we owned happens to be the most creative mind I have ever been blessed to work with. Oftentimes I found myself giving him strategies that were so tight that I could not possibly fathom he would return with concepts that were anything other than a verbatim regurgitation of the words used in the strategy statement at the creative briefing. It was during those times I felt he produced his best work. Surprising me time and time again with his creative interpretation of the strategy that always met the objective, he seemed to effortlessly choreograph a show-stopping dance routine (the campaign) for each musical (the product) that nobody else envisioned, including me (the producer).

When injecting creativity into your campaign, be cautioned not to lose the brand differentiation message. If you do, you will be a victim of the ever-so-popular "creative for creative's sake" mistake. Never lose sight of what we have covered thus far and what you have already determined for your brand positioning. If you are technically superior, explore leading with that. You have a real story, a compelling argument that is relevant to your buyer. Your job is to tell them, not to waste your precious inventory simply entertaining. Once you are an established brand and maybe even a market leader you have quite a bit more leeway, maybe. When your differentiation is superiority that can be proven, don't cloud your advantage with frivolous distractions.

If lifestyle is your differentiation, then you have more creative freedom as your goal is to emotionally connect with your prospect. Fashion advertisers often attempt to paint a picture of the 'type of people' that wear that brand. The advertising goal here is to get the prospect to identify with the models in that ad, relate to them as similar or how they wish to be perceived by others, and to ultimately buy some version of the outfit featured in the ad so they look like that, too. People sailing on a yacht, a young family playing soccer in the backyard, a couple attending the opera, friends hanging out at a bar, each of these ads intending to sell a scarf rarely attempts to explain why their scarf is a better choice than other scarfs.

What on earth do Clydesdales have to do with beer? How about a gecko's relevance to insurance beyond the similar pronunciation to the brand it represents? These are examples where greater creative leniency is possible to solidify a brand personality in the minds of the unassuming public. Tony the Tiger, Colonel Sanders, Jolly Green Giant, Pillsbury Doughboy, the Aflac Duck. These are all great examples of creative character development being used to establish brand personality and differentiation in the marketplace. In other words, manipulation. You love the character, you'll consider the brand.

Since the 1950's, a fast food chain has consistently

advertised the perceived benefit of a flame-broiled hamburger. There is no lifestyle depiction. No consumer testimonials about the hamburger eating experience and how it has changed a life or two. Yet, the advertising message lives on. Clearly and consistently. Most people know the popular fast food joints to get a good burger. Yet these advertisers continue to spend millions of dollars every year reminding us they are there and how their menu is different from the other guy. If these brands are so famous, why don't they stop advertising? Because we don't care about them, remember? We all have lives to live and we do not wake up every day thinking about these businesses and analyzing the differences between their hamburger cooking methods. We need to be reminded of their offering so they stay top of mind. When the desire for a burger arises, we recall the message we like best and we go and purchase.

No differentiation

+ no message reminder

= no sale.

True for even the most popular brands in the world.

Determining your creative approach must come from the root of your brand differentiation strategy and posture. Don't get carried away, unless you can.

Brand debut and refinement

The Cotton T-Shirt

Full on commitment time, folks. Your expert media plan depicts exactly where your bullseye customer is and your strategy is solid. The time for massive action has arrived. In other words, no whimpering in to the market. You've done the work and you are ready.

This is the period that I affectionately refer to as stirring the sauce. I love to cook and am quite proud of my Italian heritage. Over the years I have found pleasure in watching my family and friends enjoy my homemade sauce and fight over the last meatball. Actually, part of that is inaccurate. There is never a last meatball on my table to fight over. Like most Italians in my family, I always make too much food.

Up to this point, you have done the shopping, picked out all your ingredients based on your research of the perfect sauce elements, made a small test batch to identify modifications for the big day, and now the pot is on the stove. That's debut time. Once the flame is lit under the pot, you're live!

Naturally, when all ingredients enter the pot, the sauce is not finished. All day long, every single time you get anywhere near the kitchen, you stir the sauce. If you leave it unattended, it may burn. It may need more of this or that added throughout the process, so you add. All the while, you are monitoring closely and never taking your eye off the prize. With great love, care and attention, you keep giving it what it needs, even if it is just a simple stir. Do not fear refinement! You have a solid rationale for your ingredients and would never substitute

crushed tomatoes for chocolate this far into the process. However, you may find that fresh basil is a better option than dried.

While carefully managing the effectiveness of your communication strategy, beware of shiny object syndrome. This often appears as a comment or idea that suddenly appears out of nowhere and was never part of the process, yet now sounds great and makes a lot of sense to you because someone bought your product because of it. Resist the urge to abandon ship and swim over to a new one you know nothing about because the new ship may look sturdy from afar yet the hull could be filled with holes. I am not suggesting you ignore this new insight. I am simply saying that unless and until something becomes so frequent that it is too big to ignore, just take the victory (the sale) and stay on course. Naturally the moment you recognize momentum taking shape with an unexplored direction, you can inject it into the testing process. There will be many small victories that were not explored, expect them. Watch them. Evaluate them. If one becomes truly worthy of a shift, have at it, otherwise, let it be.

A critical component of debut and refinement is always watching your competition. Every single day, without fail. What they are saying, where they are saying it, how they are saying it. You are watching for product enhancements, line extensions, promotions, price changes, anything and everything they are doing. You must know the minute they do it and begin your analysis of where their strategist may be headed with it, and why. Being competitive in your market does not mean answering every step your rivals take. That is a reactive posture and is certain to dilute your brand message if you are always reacting to the other guy's message by changing the core of who you are. Your goal here is to make every effort to predict where your competitors are going so you are never taken out of the game. Appoint someone on your team to be dedicated to competitive tracking. Every time a move worthy of consideration is made, your entire team should receive an alert explaining who did what, where, and possible implications for your brand. Dedicated trackers look at everything their competitors are doing in print advertising, television, radio, internet and social media, outdoor advertising and even location signage for brick and mortar. While your tracker is alerting the team at the time of major competitive activity, they should also prepare and deliver a quarterly review presentation comprised of each competitor's noteworthy activity so predictions on future plans can be discussed.

It is important to mention that if you are the new kid on the block, the bully may take note. The bully is the established market leader. This brand has great power and influence, and although you may experience a temporary feeling of pride that you are on the radar, truth is that the competitor is not as intimidated by you as you may think. They may walk by you and try to slap you on the head (toss out a small competitive attack ad), but it is highly doubtful that they are giving you all their attention (spending their entire budget fighting you). Market leaders often have deep pockets, so they have the means to try to kick you around a bit. You, on the other hand, may not have the same budget depth so if you take the bait and get caught up in an ad war with the giant, you may get squashed because of your distraction. Your demise would be found in your decision to not only stop aiming your communication at your bullseye, but not aiming your communication anywhere on the target at all because you are consumed with talking to your competitor. You can't hit a target you are not aiming for.

Didn't your mother tell you that the best way to deal with a bully is to ignore them? In cases like this, she would be right. Again, just in cases like this. If you really do have the goods, in other words if you really are superior, then come out swinging. If you opt to engage, you must be ready.

How to use this guide

In the same manner that a therapist may write a guide outlining suggested coping methods for a particular disorder, this guide is intended to do the same. In no way am I diagnosing your situation or recommending a specific treatment. We have never spoken to each other therefore I know nothing about you.

By now my hope is that you have an understanding of the basic steps in the brand differentiation process so you know what to expect and possibly consider as you prepare for your consultation with the marketing doctor you ultimately choose to conduct your product's thorough physical exam. Be educated so you understand the treatment plan that will be recommended and stay actively engaged in it, asking the right questions all the way through.

As this series name suggests, it is very likely that you read through this guide within 60-minutes and hopefully did so cover to cover in one sitting. Your mind may be racing with thoughts and that is exactly what was supposed to happen. Write them down, all in one place. Keep it with you so whenever a new thought appears, you can add it. Spend a few days allowing the thoughts and ideas to keep barreling in.

After that, read this again, cover to cover, one sitting. Go back and read all the thoughts and ideas you have recorded. You should find that you will now cross some off, add some new ones, and further expand on others that appear to have the strongest legs. You should see clear paths start to evolve at this stage of the process.

The time has arrived to start a fresh page, and begin constructing your brand development plan.

I encourage you to revisit this guide throughout the process, refreshing with the section that discusses the phase you are in, as well as the one you are heading to next, then stop, and execute. There are two main reasons for this suggestion. First, although this guide was prepared to be a quick read for you, there is a lot to retain and consider, especially the warnings to avoid the common pitfalls that have been discussed. They deserve your attention at the appropriate time when you are approaching the phase in which they typically occur. Second, you will become more sophisticated as you progress through this process and as you read certain sections again, it is highly probable that you will read the information through a different lens in the coming weeks. More ideas will continue to come to you, and they may be stronger than the ones you have today.

Brand differentiation is a fluid process. Your competitors will keep moving forward so you cannot remain static or your strategy of today will be addressing market conditions that no longer exist. Keep stirring the sauce, and I will too. I expect to be wearing your brand's cotton t-shirt while I do.

The Cotton T-Shirt

About the Author

Lori Thomas began her advertising career over 25 years ago in Manhattan. She has developed and executed strategic marketing campaigns across a myriad of industries for small mom-and-pop shops through international giants. She is a former adjunct instructor of marketing for the State University of New York, and the founder of several successful businesses including a 17-year run as the co-founder of a national advertising agency that had offices in Manhattan and Long Island. Married with a son and a step-daughter, she can regularly be found jet-setting between New York and Florida with her 13-year old Pomeranian, Bling.

60-MINUTE MARKETING

THE COTTON T-SHIRT

A beginner's guide to developing a breakout brand

LORI THOMAS

60-MINUTE MARKETING

BULLS EYE

A beginner's guide to customer targeting and media

LORI THOMAS

60-MINUTE MARKETING

THE
DANCE

A beginner's guide to creating show-stopping ads

LORI THOMAS

www.ingramcontent.com/pod-product-compliance
Lightning Source LLC
Chambersburg PA
CBHW071242220526
45468CB00002B/972